BIRD WATCHING

J O U R N A L

THIS BOOK BELONGS TO:

_____

_____

INDEX

PAGE	DATE	SIGHTINGS

INDEX

PAGE	DATE	SIGHTINGS

INDEX

PAGE	DATE	SIGHTINGS

INDEX

PAGE	DATE	SIGHTINGS

INDEX

PAGE	DATE	SIGHTINGS

INDEX

PAGE	DATE	SIGHTINGS

ᴥᴥᴥᴥ WATCHING LOG ᴥᴥᴥᴥ

LOCATION:

GPS:

DATE:

TIME: AM ○ PM ○

WEATHER:

TEMPERATURE:

BIRD NAME / TYPE:

BIRD COLORS:

SIGHTINGS:

MY ACTIONS:

PHOTO / SKETCH:

NOTES:

WATCHING LOG

LOCATION:

GPS:

DATE:

TIME: AM ◯ PM ◯

WEATHER:

TEMPERATURE:

BIRD NAME / TYPE:

BIRD COLORS:

SIGHTINGS:

MY ACTIONS:

PHOTO / SKETCH:

NOTES:

WATCHING LOG

LOCATION:

GPS:

DATE:

TIME: AM ○ PM ○

WEATHER:

TEMPERATURE:

BIRD NAME / TYPE:

BIRD COLORS:

SIGHTINGS:

MY ACTIONS:

PHOTO / SKETCH:

NOTES:

WATCHING LOG

LOCATION:

GPS:

DATE:

TIME: AM ○ PM ○

WEATHER:

TEMPERATURE:

BIRD NAME / TYPE:

BIRD COLORS:

SIGHTINGS:

MY ACTIONS:

PHOTO / SKETCH:

NOTES:

WATCHING LOG

LOCATION:

GPS:

DATE:

TIME: AM ○ PM ○

WEATHER:

TEMPERATURE:

BIRD NAME / TYPE:

BIRD COLORS:

SIGHTINGS:

MY ACTIONS:

PHOTO / SKETCH:

NOTES:

WATCHING LOG

LOCATION:

GPS:

DATE:

TIME: AM ○ PM ○

WEATHER:

TEMPERATURE:

BIRD NAME / TYPE:

BIRD COLORS:

SIGHTINGS:

MY ACTIONS:

PHOTO / SKETCH:

NOTES:

✦✦✦✦✦✦ WATCHING LOG ✦✦✦✦✦✦

LOCATION:

GPS:

DATE:

TIME: AM ○   PM ○

WEATHER:

TEMPERATURE:

BIRD NAME / TYPE:

BIRD COLORS:

SIGHTINGS:

MY ACTIONS:

PHOTO / SKETCH:

NOTES:

WATCHING LOG

LOCATION:

GPS:

DATE:

TIME: AM ○ PM ○

WEATHER:

TEMPERATURE:

BIRD NAME / TYPE:

BIRD COLORS:

SIGHTINGS:

MY ACTIONS:

PHOTO / SKETCH:

NOTES:

WATCHING LOG

LOCATION:

GPS:

DATE:

TIME: AM ○ PM ○

WEATHER:

TEMPERATURE:

BIRD NAME / TYPE:

BIRD COLORS:

SIGHTINGS:

MY ACTIONS:

PHOTO / SKETCH:

NOTES:

WATCHING LOG

LOCATION:

GPS:

DATE:

TIME:　　　　AM ○　PM ○

WEATHER:

TEMPERATURE:

BIRD NAME / TYPE:

BIRD COLORS:

SIGHTINGS:

MY ACTIONS:

PHOTO / SKETCH:

NOTES:

WATCHING LOG

LOCATION:

GPS:

DATE:

TIME: AM ○ PM ○

WEATHER:

TEMPERATURE:

BIRD NAME / TYPE:

BIRD COLORS:

SIGHTINGS:

MY ACTIONS:

PHOTO / SKETCH:

NOTES:

WATCHING LOG

LOCATION:

GPS:

DATE:

TIME: AM ○   PM ○

WEATHER:

TEMPERATURE:

BIRD NAME / TYPE:

BIRD COLORS:

SIGHTINGS:

MY ACTIONS:

PHOTO / SKETCH:

NOTES:

WATCHING LOG

LOCATION:

GPS:

DATE:

TIME: AM○ PM○

WEATHER:

TEMPERATURE:

BIRD NAME / TYPE:

BIRD COLORS:

SIGHTINGS:

MY ACTIONS:

PHOTO / SKETCH:

NOTES:

WATCHING LOG

LOCATION:

GPS:

DATE:

TIME: AM ○ PM ○

WEATHER:

TEMPERATURE:

BIRD NAME / TYPE:

BIRD COLORS:

SIGHTINGS:

MY ACTIONS:

PHOTO / SKETCH:

NOTES:

WATCHING LOG

LOCATION:

GPS:

DATE:

TIME: AM ○ PM ○

WEATHER:

TEMPERATURE:

BIRD NAME / TYPE:

BIRD COLORS:

SIGHTINGS:

MY ACTIONS:

PHOTO / SKETCH:

NOTES:

WATCHING LOG

LOCATION:

GPS:

DATE:

TIME: AM ○ PM ○

WEATHER:

TEMPERATURE:

BIRD NAME / TYPE:

BIRD COLORS:

SIGHTINGS:

MY ACTIONS:

PHOTO / SKETCH:

NOTES:

WATCHING LOG

LOCATION:

GPS:

DATE:

TIME: AM ○ PM ○

WEATHER:

TEMPERATURE:

BIRD NAME / TYPE:

BIRD COLORS:

SIGHTINGS:

MY ACTIONS:

PHOTO / SKETCH:

NOTES:

WATCHING LOG

LOCATION:

GPS:

DATE:

TIME: AM ○ PM ○

WEATHER:

TEMPERATURE:

BIRD NAME / TYPE:

BIRD COLORS:

SIGHTINGS:

MY ACTIONS:

PHOTO / SKETCH:

NOTES:

WATCHING LOG

LOCATION:

GPS:

DATE:

TIME: AM ○ PM ○

WEATHER:

TEMPERATURE:

BIRD NAME / TYPE:

BIRD COLORS:

SIGHTINGS:

MY ACTIONS:

PHOTO / SKETCH:

NOTES:

WATCHING LOG

LOCATION:

GPS:

DATE:

TIME: AM ○ PM ○

WEATHER:

TEMPERATURE:

BIRD NAME / TYPE:

BIRD COLORS:

SIGHTINGS:

MY ACTIONS:

PHOTO / SKETCH:

NOTES:

◆┼┼┼┼┼◆ WATCHING LOG ◆┼┼┼┼┼◆

LOCATION:

GPS:

DATE:

TIME: AM ○ PM ○

WEATHER:

TEMPERATURE:

BIRD NAME / TYPE:

BIRD COLORS:

SIGHTINGS:

MY ACTIONS:

PHOTO / SKETCH:

NOTES:

WATCHING LOG

LOCATION:

GPS:

DATE:

TIME: AM ○ PM ○

WEATHER:

TEMPERATURE:

BIRD NAME / TYPE:

BIRD COLORS:

SIGHTINGS:

MY ACTIONS:

PHOTO / SKETCH:

NOTES:

WATCHING LOG

LOCATION:

GPS:

DATE:

TIME: AM ○ PM ○

WEATHER:

TEMPERATURE:

BIRD NAME / TYPE:

BIRD COLORS:

SIGHTINGS:

MY ACTIONS:

PHOTO / SKETCH:

NOTES:

WATCHING LOG

LOCATION:

GPS:

DATE:

TIME: AM ○ PM ○

WEATHER:

TEMPERATURE:

BIRD NAME / TYPE:

BIRD COLORS:

SIGHTINGS:

MY ACTIONS:

PHOTO / SKETCH:

NOTES:

WATCHING LOG

LOCATION:

GPS:

DATE:

TIME: AM ○ PM ○

WEATHER:

TEMPERATURE:

BIRD NAME / TYPE:

BIRD COLORS:

SIGHTINGS:

MY ACTIONS:

PHOTO / SKETCH:

NOTES:

WATCHING LOG

LOCATION:

GPS:

DATE:

TIME: AM ○   PM ○

WEATHER:

TEMPERATURE:

BIRD NAME / TYPE:

BIRD COLORS:

SIGHTINGS:

MY ACTIONS:

PHOTO / SKETCH:

NOTES:

WATCHING LOG

LOCATION:

GPS:

DATE:

TIME: AM ○ PM ○

WEATHER:

TEMPERATURE:

BIRD NAME / TYPE:

BIRD COLORS:

SIGHTINGS:

MY ACTIONS:

PHOTO / SKETCH:

NOTES:

WATCHING LOG

LOCATION:

GPS:

DATE:

TIME: AM ○   PM ○

WEATHER:

TEMPERATURE:

BIRD NAME / TYPE:

BIRD COLORS:

SIGHTINGS:

MY ACTIONS:

PHOTO / SKETCH:

NOTES:

WATCHING LOG

LOCATION:

GPS:

DATE:

TIME: AM ○ PM ○

WEATHER:

TEMPERATURE:

BIRD NAME / TYPE:

BIRD COLORS:

SIGHTINGS:

MY ACTIONS:

PHOTO / SKETCH:

NOTES:

WATCHING LOG

LOCATION:

GPS:

DATE:

TIME: AM ○ PM ○

WEATHER:

TEMPERATURE:

BIRD NAME / TYPE:

BIRD COLORS:

SIGHTINGS:

MY ACTIONS:

PHOTO / SKETCH:

NOTES:

✦✦✦✦✦ WATCHING LOG ✦✦✦✦✦

LOCATION:

GPS:

DATE:

TIME: AM ○   PM ○

WEATHER:

TEMPERATURE:

BIRD NAME / TYPE:

BIRD COLORS:

SIGHTINGS:

MY ACTIONS:

PHOTO / SKETCH:

NOTES:

WATCHING LOG

LOCATION:

GPS:

DATE:

TIME: AM ○ PM ○

WEATHER:

TEMPERATURE:

BIRD NAME / TYPE:

BIRD COLORS:

SIGHTINGS:

MY ACTIONS:

PHOTO / SKETCH:

NOTES:

WATCHING LOG

LOCATION:

GPS:

DATE:

TIME: AM ○ PM ○

WEATHER:

TEMPERATURE:

BIRD NAME / TYPE:

BIRD COLORS:

SIGHTINGS:

MY ACTIONS:

PHOTO / SKETCH:

NOTES:

WATCHING LOG

LOCATION:

GPS:

DATE:

TIME: AM ○   PM ○

WEATHER:

TEMPERATURE:

BIRD NAME / TYPE:

BIRD COLORS:

SIGHTINGS:

MY ACTIONS:

PHOTO / SKETCH:

NOTES:

WATCHING LOG

LOCATION:

GPS:

DATE:

TIME: AM ○ PM ○

WEATHER:

TEMPERATURE:

BIRD NAME / TYPE:

BIRD COLORS:

SIGHTINGS:

MY ACTIONS:

PHOTO / SKETCH:

NOTES:

WATCHING LOG

LOCATION:

GPS:

DATE:

TIME: AM ○   PM ○

WEATHER:

TEMPERATURE:

BIRD NAME / TYPE:

BIRD COLORS:

SIGHTINGS:

MY ACTIONS:

PHOTO / SKETCH:

NOTES:

WATCHING LOG

LOCATION:

GPS:

DATE:

TIME: AM ○ PM ○

WEATHER:

TEMPERATURE:

BIRD NAME / TYPE:

BIRD COLORS:

SIGHTINGS:

MY ACTIONS:

PHOTO / SKETCH:

NOTES:

WATCHING LOG

LOCATION:

GPS:

DATE:

TIME: AM ○ PM ○

WEATHER:

TEMPERATURE:

BIRD NAME / TYPE:

BIRD COLORS:

SIGHTINGS:

MY ACTIONS:

PHOTO / SKETCH:

NOTES:

WATCHING LOG

LOCATION:

GPS:

DATE:

TIME: AM ○ PM ○

WEATHER:

TEMPERATURE:

BIRD NAME / TYPE:

BIRD COLORS:

SIGHTINGS:

MY ACTIONS:

PHOTO / SKETCH:

NOTES:

WATCHING LOG

LOCATION:

GPS:

DATE:

TIME: AM ○ PM ○

WEATHER:

TEMPERATURE:

BIRD NAME / TYPE:

BIRD COLORS:

SIGHTINGS:

MY ACTIONS:

PHOTO / SKETCH:

NOTES:

✦✦✦✦✦ **WATCHING LOG** ✦✦✦✦✦

LOCATION:

GPS:

DATE:

TIME: AM ○ PM ○

WEATHER:

TEMPERATURE:

BIRD NAME / TYPE:

BIRD COLORS:

SIGHTINGS:

MY ACTIONS:

PHOTO / SKETCH:

NOTES:

WATCHING LOG

LOCATION:

GPS:

DATE:

TIME: AM ○ PM ○

WEATHER:

TEMPERATURE:

BIRD NAME / TYPE:

BIRD COLORS:

SIGHTINGS:

MY ACTIONS:

PHOTO / SKETCH:

NOTES:

WATCHING LOG

LOCATION:

GPS:

DATE:

TIME: AM ○ PM ○

WEATHER:

TEMPERATURE:

BIRD NAME / TYPE:

BIRD COLORS:

SIGHTINGS:

MY ACTIONS:

PHOTO / SKETCH:

NOTES:

WATCHING LOG

LOCATION:

GPS:

DATE:

TIME: AM ○ PM ○

WEATHER:

TEMPERATURE:

BIRD NAME / TYPE:

BIRD COLORS:

SIGHTINGS:

MY ACTIONS:

PHOTO / SKETCH:

NOTES:

WATCHING LOG

LOCATION:

GPS:

DATE:

TIME: AM ○   PM ○

WEATHER:

TEMPERATURE:

BIRD NAME / TYPE:

BIRD COLORS:

SIGHTINGS:

MY ACTIONS:

PHOTO / SKETCH:

NOTES:

WATCHING LOG

LOCATION:

GPS:

DATE:

TIME: AM ○ PM ○

WEATHER:

TEMPERATURE:

BIRD NAME / TYPE:

BIRD COLORS:

SIGHTINGS:

MY ACTIONS:

PHOTO / SKETCH:

NOTES:

WATCHING LOG

LOCATION:

GPS:

DATE:

TIME: AM ○ PM ○

WEATHER:

TEMPERATURE:

BIRD NAME / TYPE:

BIRD COLORS:

SIGHTINGS:

MY ACTIONS:

PHOTO / SKETCH:

NOTES:

WATCHING LOG

LOCATION:

GPS:

DATE:

TIME: AM ○ PM ○

WEATHER:

TEMPERATURE:

BIRD NAME / TYPE:

BIRD COLORS:

SIGHTINGS:

MY ACTIONS:

PHOTO / SKETCH:

NOTES:

WATCHING LOG

LOCATION:

GPS:

DATE:

TIME: AM ○   PM ○

WEATHER:

TEMPERATURE:

BIRD NAME / TYPE:

BIRD COLORS:

SIGHTINGS:

MY ACTIONS:

PHOTO / SKETCH:

NOTES:

WATCHING LOG

LOCATION:

GPS:

DATE:

TIME: AM ○   PM ○

WEATHER:

TEMPERATURE:

BIRD NAME / TYPE:

BIRD COLORS:

SIGHTINGS:

MY ACTIONS:

PHOTO / SKETCH:

NOTES:

WATCHING LOG

LOCATION:

GPS:

DATE:

TIME: AM ○ PM ○

WEATHER:

TEMPERATURE:

BIRD NAME / TYPE:

BIRD COLORS:

SIGHTINGS:

MY ACTIONS:

PHOTO / SKETCH:

NOTES:

WATCHING LOG

LOCATION:

GPS:

DATE:

TIME: AM ○ PM ○

WEATHER:

TEMPERATURE:

BIRD NAME / TYPE:

BIRD COLORS:

SIGHTINGS:

MY ACTIONS:

PHOTO / SKETCH:

NOTES:

WATCHING LOG

LOCATION:

GPS:

DATE:

TIME: AM ○ PM ○

WEATHER:

TEMPERATURE:

BIRD NAME / TYPE:

BIRD COLORS:

SIGHTINGS:

MY ACTIONS:

PHOTO / SKETCH:

NOTES:

WATCHING LOG

LOCATION:

GPS:

DATE:

TIME: AM○ PM○

WEATHER:

TEMPERATURE:

BIRD NAME / TYPE:

BIRD COLORS:

SIGHTINGS:

MY ACTIONS:

PHOTO / SKETCH:

NOTES:

WATCHING LOG

LOCATION:

GPS:

DATE:

TIME: AM◯ PM◯

WEATHER:

TEMPERATURE:

BIRD NAME / TYPE:

BIRD COLORS:

SIGHTINGS:

MY ACTIONS:

PHOTO / SKETCH:

NOTES:

WATCHING LOG

LOCATION:

GPS:

DATE:

TIME: AM ○ PM ○

WEATHER:

TEMPERATURE:

BIRD NAME / TYPE:

BIRD COLORS:

SIGHTINGS:

MY ACTIONS:

PHOTO / SKETCH:

NOTES:

WATCHING LOG

LOCATION:

GPS:

DATE:

TIME: AM ○ PM ○

WEATHER:

TEMPERATURE:

BIRD NAME / TYPE:

BIRD COLORS:

SIGHTINGS:

MY ACTIONS:

PHOTO / SKETCH:

NOTES:

WATCHING LOG

LOCATION:

GPS:

DATE:

TIME: AM ○ PM ○

WEATHER:

TEMPERATURE:

BIRD NAME / TYPE:

BIRD COLORS:

SIGHTINGS:

MY ACTIONS:

PHOTO / SKETCH:

NOTES:

WATCHING LOG

LOCATION:

GPS:

DATE:

TIME: AM ○   PM ○

WEATHER:

TEMPERATURE:

BIRD NAME / TYPE:

BIRD COLORS:

SIGHTINGS:

MY ACTIONS:

PHOTO / SKETCH:

NOTES:

WATCHING LOG

LOCATION:

GPS:

DATE:

TIME: AM ○ PM ○

WEATHER:

TEMPERATURE:

BIRD NAME / TYPE:

BIRD COLORS:

SIGHTINGS:

MY ACTIONS:

PHOTO / SKETCH:

NOTES:

WATCHING LOG

LOCATION:

GPS:

DATE:

TIME: AM ○ PM ○

WEATHER:

TEMPERATURE:

BIRD NAME / TYPE:

BIRD COLORS:

SIGHTINGS:

MY ACTIONS:

PHOTO / SKETCH:

NOTES:

WATCHING LOG

LOCATION:

GPS:

DATE:

TIME: AM ○ PM ○

WEATHER:

TEMPERATURE:

BIRD NAME / TYPE:

BIRD COLORS:

SIGHTINGS:

MY ACTIONS:

PHOTO / SKETCH:

NOTES:

WATCHING LOG

LOCATION:

GPS:

DATE:

TIME: AM◯ PM◯

WEATHER:

TEMPERATURE:

BIRD NAME / TYPE:

BIRD COLORS:

SIGHTINGS:

MY ACTIONS:

PHOTO / SKETCH:

NOTES:

WATCHING LOG

LOCATION:

GPS:

DATE:

TIME: AM ○ PM ○

WEATHER:

TEMPERATURE:

BIRD NAME / TYPE:

BIRD COLORS:

SIGHTINGS:

MY ACTIONS:

PHOTO / SKETCH:

NOTES:

WATCHING LOG

LOCATION:

GPS:

DATE:

TIME: AM ○ PM ○

WEATHER:

TEMPERATURE:

BIRD NAME / TYPE:

BIRD COLORS:

SIGHTINGS:

MY ACTIONS:

PHOTO / SKETCH:

NOTES:

WATCHING LOG

LOCATION:

GPS:

DATE:

TIME: AM ○ PM ○

WEATHER:

TEMPERATURE:

BIRD NAME / TYPE:

BIRD COLORS:

SIGHTINGS:

MY ACTIONS:

PHOTO / SKETCH:

NOTES:

WATCHING LOG

LOCATION:

GPS:

DATE:

TIME: AM ○ PM ○

WEATHER:

TEMPERATURE:

BIRD NAME / TYPE:

BIRD COLORS:

SIGHTINGS:

MY ACTIONS:

PHOTO / SKETCH:

NOTES:

WATCHING LOG

LOCATION:

GPS:

DATE:

TIME: AM ○ PM ○

WEATHER:

TEMPERATURE:

BIRD NAME / TYPE:

BIRD COLORS:

SIGHTINGS:

MY ACTIONS:

PHOTO / SKETCH:

NOTES:

WATCHING LOG

LOCATION:

GPS:

DATE:

TIME: AM ○ PM ○

WEATHER:

TEMPERATURE:

BIRD NAME / TYPE:

BIRD COLORS:

SIGHTINGS:

MY ACTIONS:

PHOTO / SKETCH:

NOTES:

WATCHING LOG

LOCATION:

GPS:

DATE:

TIME: AM ○ PM ○

WEATHER:

TEMPERATURE:

BIRD NAME / TYPE:

BIRD COLORS:

SIGHTINGS:

MY ACTIONS:

PHOTO / SKETCH:

NOTES:

WATCHING LOG

LOCATION:

GPS:

DATE:

TIME: AM ○ PM ○

WEATHER:

TEMPERATURE:

BIRD NAME / TYPE:

BIRD COLORS:

SIGHTINGS:

MY ACTIONS:

PHOTO / SKETCH:

NOTES:

WATCHING LOG

LOCATION:

GPS:

DATE:

TIME: AM ○ PM ○

WEATHER:

TEMPERATURE:

BIRD NAME / TYPE:

BIRD COLORS:

SIGHTINGS:

MY ACTIONS:

PHOTO / SKETCH:

NOTES:

WATCHING LOG

LOCATION:

GPS:

DATE:

TIME: AM ○   PM ○

WEATHER:

TEMPERATURE:

BIRD NAME / TYPE:

BIRD COLORS:

SIGHTINGS:

MY ACTIONS:

PHOTO / SKETCH:

NOTES:

WATCHING LOG

LOCATION:

GPS:

DATE:

TIME: AM ○ PM ○

WEATHER:

TEMPERATURE:

BIRD NAME / TYPE:

BIRD COLORS:

SIGHTINGS:

MY ACTIONS:

PHOTO / SKETCH:

NOTES:

WATCHING LOG

LOCATION:

GPS:

DATE:

TIME: AM ○ PM ○

WEATHER:

TEMPERATURE:

BIRD NAME / TYPE:

BIRD COLORS:

SIGHTINGS:

MY ACTIONS:

PHOTO / SKETCH:

NOTES:

WATCHING LOG

LOCATION:

GPS:

DATE:

TIME: AM ○   PM ○

WEATHER:

TEMPERATURE:

BIRD NAME / TYPE:

BIRD COLORS:

SIGHTINGS:

MY ACTIONS:

PHOTO / SKETCH:

NOTES:

WATCHING LOG

LOCATION:

GPS:

DATE:

TIME: AM○ PM○

WEATHER:

TEMPERATURE:

BIRD NAME / TYPE:

BIRD COLORS:

SIGHTINGS:

MY ACTIONS:

PHOTO / SKETCH:

NOTES:

WATCHING LOG

LOCATION:

GPS:

DATE:

TIME: AM ○ PM ○

WEATHER:

TEMPERATURE:

BIRD NAME / TYPE:

BIRD COLORS:

SIGHTINGS:

MY ACTIONS:

PHOTO / SKETCH:

NOTES:

WATCHING LOG

LOCATION:

GPS:

DATE:

TIME: AM ○ PM ○

WEATHER:

TEMPERATURE:

BIRD NAME / TYPE:

BIRD COLORS:

SIGHTINGS:

MY ACTIONS:

PHOTO / SKETCH:

NOTES:

WATCHING LOG

LOCATION:

GPS:

DATE:

TIME: AM ○ PM ○

WEATHER:

TEMPERATURE:

BIRD NAME / TYPE:

BIRD COLORS:

SIGHTINGS:

MY ACTIONS:

PHOTO / SKETCH:

NOTES:

WATCHING LOG

LOCATION:

GPS:

DATE:

TIME: AM ○ PM ○

WEATHER:

TEMPERATURE:

BIRD NAME / TYPE:

BIRD COLORS:

SIGHTINGS:

MY ACTIONS:

PHOTO / SKETCH:

NOTES:

WATCHING LOG

LOCATION:

GPS:

DATE:

TIME: AM ○ PM ○

WEATHER:

TEMPERATURE:

BIRD NAME / TYPE:

BIRD COLORS:

SIGHTINGS:

MY ACTIONS:

PHOTO / SKETCH:

NOTES:

WATCHING LOG

LOCATION:

GPS:

DATE:

TIME: AM ○ PM ○

WEATHER:

TEMPERATURE:

BIRD NAME / TYPE:

BIRD COLORS:

SIGHTINGS:

MY ACTIONS:

PHOTO / SKETCH:

NOTES:

WATCHING LOG

LOCATION:

GPS:

DATE:

TIME: AM ○ PM ○

WEATHER:

TEMPERATURE:

BIRD NAME / TYPE:

BIRD COLORS:

SIGHTINGS:

MY ACTIONS:

PHOTO / SKETCH:

NOTES:

◆┼┼┼┼ ◆ WATCHING LOG ◆┼┼┼┼ ◆

LOCATION:

GPS:

DATE:

TIME: AM ○ PM ○

WEATHER:

TEMPERATURE:

BIRD NAME / TYPE:

BIRD COLORS:

SIGHTINGS:

MY ACTIONS:

PHOTO / SKETCH:

NOTES:

WATCHING LOG

LOCATION:

GPS:

DATE:

TIME: AM ○ PM ○

WEATHER:

TEMPERATURE:

BIRD NAME / TYPE:

BIRD COLORS:

SIGHTINGS:

MY ACTIONS:

PHOTO / SKETCH:

NOTES:

WATCHING LOG

LOCATION:

GPS:

DATE:

TIME: AM ○ PM ○

WEATHER:

TEMPERATURE:

BIRD NAME / TYPE:

BIRD COLORS:

SIGHTINGS:

MY ACTIONS:

PHOTO / SKETCH:

NOTES:

WATCHING LOG

LOCATION:

GPS:

DATE:

TIME: AM ○   PM ○

WEATHER:

TEMPERATURE:

BIRD NAME / TYPE:

BIRD COLORS:

SIGHTINGS:

MY ACTIONS:

PHOTO / SKETCH:

NOTES:

WATCHING LOG

LOCATION:

GPS:

DATE:

TIME: AM ○   PM ○

WEATHER:

TEMPERATURE:

BIRD NAME / TYPE:

BIRD COLORS:

SIGHTINGS:

MY ACTIONS:

PHOTO / SKETCH:

NOTES:

WATCHING LOG

LOCATION:

GPS:

DATE:

TIME: AM ○ PM ○

WEATHER:

TEMPERATURE:

BIRD NAME / TYPE:

BIRD COLORS:

SIGHTINGS:

MY ACTIONS:

PHOTO / SKETCH:

NOTES:

WATCHING LOG

LOCATION:

GPS:

DATE:

TIME: AM ○ PM ○

WEATHER:

TEMPERATURE:

BIRD NAME / TYPE:

BIRD COLORS:

SIGHTINGS:

MY ACTIONS:

PHOTO / SKETCH:

NOTES:

WATCHING LOG

LOCATION:

GPS:

DATE:

TIME: AM○ PM○

WEATHER:

TEMPERATURE:

BIRD NAME / TYPE:

BIRD COLORS:

SIGHTINGS:

MY ACTIONS:

PHOTO / SKETCH:

NOTES:

WATCHING LOG

LOCATION:

GPS:

DATE:

TIME: AM ○ PM ○

WEATHER:

TEMPERATURE:

BIRD NAME / TYPE:

BIRD COLORS:

SIGHTINGS:

MY ACTIONS:

PHOTO / SKETCH:

NOTES:

WATCHING LOG

LOCATION:

GPS:

DATE:

TIME: AM ○ PM ○

WEATHER:

TEMPERATURE:

BIRD NAME / TYPE:

BIRD COLORS:

SIGHTINGS:

MY ACTIONS:

PHOTO / SKETCH:

NOTES:

WATCHING LOG

LOCATION:

GPS:

DATE:

TIME: AM ○ PM ○

WEATHER:

TEMPERATURE:

BIRD NAME / TYPE:

BIRD COLORS:

SIGHTINGS:

MY ACTIONS:

PHOTO / SKETCH:

NOTES:

WATCHING LOG

LOCATION:

GPS:

DATE:

TIME: AM ○ PM ○

WEATHER:

TEMPERATURE:

BIRD NAME / TYPE:

BIRD COLORS:

SIGHTINGS:

MY ACTIONS:

PHOTO / SKETCH:

NOTES:

WATCHING LOG

LOCATION:

GPS:

DATE:

TIME: AM ○ PM ○

WEATHER:

TEMPERATURE:

BIRD NAME / TYPE:

BIRD COLORS:

SIGHTINGS:

MY ACTIONS:

PHOTO / SKETCH:

NOTES:

WATCHING LOG

LOCATION:

GPS:

DATE:

TIME: AM ○ PM ○

WEATHER:

TEMPERATURE:

BIRD NAME / TYPE:

BIRD COLORS:

SIGHTINGS:

MY ACTIONS:

PHOTO / SKETCH:

NOTES:

WATCHING LOG

LOCATION:

GPS:

DATE:

TIME: AM ○   PM ○

WEATHER:

TEMPERATURE:

BIRD NAME / TYPE:

BIRD COLORS:

SIGHTINGS:

MY ACTIONS:

PHOTO / SKETCH:

NOTES:

WATCHING LOG

LOCATION:

GPS:

DATE:

TIME: AM ○ PM ○

WEATHER:

TEMPERATURE:

BIRD NAME / TYPE:

BIRD COLORS:

SIGHTINGS:

MY ACTIONS:

PHOTO / SKETCH:

NOTES:

✦✦✦✦✦ WATCHING LOG ✦✦✦✦✦

LOCATION:

GPS:

DATE:

TIME:　　　　AM ○　PM ○

WEATHER:

TEMPERATURE:

BIRD NAME / TYPE:

BIRD COLORS:

SIGHTINGS:

MY ACTIONS:

PHOTO / SKETCH:

NOTES:

WATCHING LOG

LOCATION:

GPS:

DATE:

TIME: AM ○ PM ○

WEATHER:

TEMPERATURE:

BIRD NAME / TYPE:

BIRD COLORS:

SIGHTINGS:

MY ACTIONS:

PHOTO / SKETCH:

NOTES:

✦✦✦✦✦✦ WATCHING LOG ✦✦✦✦✦✦

LOCATION:

GPS:

DATE:

TIME:　　　　　AM ○　PM ○

WEATHER:

TEMPERATURE:

BIRD NAME / TYPE:

BIRD COLORS:

SIGHTINGS:

MY ACTIONS:

PHOTO / SKETCH:

NOTES:

Printed in Great Britain
by Amazon

31121784R00062